TIME
FOR KIDS

A Day in
the Life of a

FIREFIGHTER

Diana Herweck

Consultant

Timothy Rasinski, Ph.D.
Kent State University

Joe Garcia
Firefighter and Paramedic
Orange County, California

Publishing Credits

Dona Herweck Rice, *Editor-in-Chief*

Robin Erickson, *Production Director*

Lee Aucoin, *Creative Director*

Conni Medina, M.A.Ed., *Editorial Director*

Jamey Acosta, *Editor*

Heidi Kellenberger, *Editor*

Lexa Hoang, *Designer*

Lesley Palmer, *Designer*

Stephanie Reid, *Photo Editor*

Rachelle Cracchiolo, M.S.Ed., *Publisher*

Based on writing from *TIME For Kids*.

TIME For Kids and the *TIME For Kids* logo are registered trademarks of TIME Inc. Used under license.

Teacher Created Materials

5301 Oceanus Drive
Huntington Beach, CA 92649-1030
http://www.tcmpub.com

ISBN 978-1-4333-3651-5

© 2012 Teacher Created Materials, Inc.

Table of Contents

On the Way!

"RRRrrr RRRrrr!" the fire truck cries as it races down the street. Everyone makes way. The **firefighters** are on their way to put out a fire. They are the heroes of the day.

Bucket Brigade

The first "fire trucks" in the 1600s were made of tubs on long poles, wheels, or sled runners. Firefighters put out fires using a **bucket brigade**. They lined up, filled buckets from the tub, and passed the buckets along the line. The last person in line threw the water on the fire.

This 1809 bucket brigade is similar to the one described in the text above. But rather than a tub at one end, they used a water pump.

Getting Ready

Firefighters are very busy. They can be called to a fire at any time of day or night. They must be ready at all times in case of an **emergency**.

▲ a controlled-burn training exercise

the kitchen ➤ in the fire station

Some firefighters live part of the time at the fire station. They pack their things, leave their families at home, and go to the fire station. They have beds, bathrooms, and a kitchen there. They also have rooms for relaxing. If there is no fire, they get to sleep at night.

▼ relaxing in the fire station lunchroom

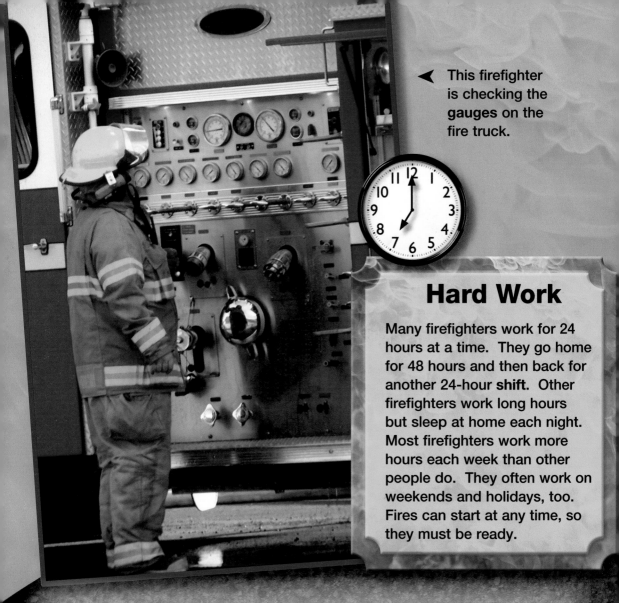

◀ This firefighter is checking the gauges on the fire truck.

Hard Work

Many firefighters work for 24 hours at a time. They go home for 48 hours and then back for another 24-hour **shift**. Other firefighters work long hours but sleep at home each night. Most firefighters work more hours each week than other people do. They often work on weekends and holidays, too. Fires can start at any time, so they must be ready.

When the firefighters are settled at the station, they check the **equipment** and the fire trucks. They check the **nozzles** on the hoses to be sure they are clear and working. They check the engine to be sure there is enough gas and oil. They must also make sure there is air in the tires.

A Firefighter's Day

A firefighter's day might look something like this.

7:00 A.M.	Wake up, eat breakfast, and head to the fire station.
8:00 A.M.	Arrive at the station.
8:30 A.M.	Walk through the station and check the equipment.
11:00 A.M.	Do a safety presentation at an elementary school.
12:00 P.M.	Eat lunch at the station.
1:00 P.M.	Check for fire safety at a local restaurant.
1:30 P.M.	Do training exercises.
3:30 P.M.	The alarm goes off. An emergency can happen at any time!
5:30 P.M.	Go back to the station. Clean and check the equipment.
6:30 P.M.	Take a shower.
7:00 P.M.	Eat dinner and relax.
10:00 P.M.	Go to bed. Be ready if another call comes in.

A Busy Day

There are many different emergencies besides fires. Sometimes, firefighters are called to help people in medical emergencies. Sometimes, they **rescue** people who are trapped or in **danger**. Other times, they clear areas near fires or other disasters. They help people after earthquakes, terrible storms, and crashes, too. And, firefighters spend many hours working to prevent fires from starting.

Firefighters are almost always working, even if there are no fires. They go to schools to teach about fire safety. They study to be sure they are good at their jobs. They practice putting out fires so they are ready when a fire comes.

The History of Firefighting			
24 BC	**about 1500**	**1648**	**1672**
Roman emperor Augustus makes laws for checking and preventing fires and pays the first firefighters.	The first fire pump is used.	The first public fire department is formed in New Amsterdam (now New York) by volunteers.	Leather hoses and couplings for connecting hoses are used for the first time.

A firefighter teaches fire safety to elementary school children. ▼

Training

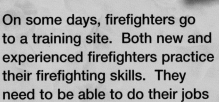

On some days, firefighters go to a training site. Both new and experienced firefighters practice their firefighting skills. They need to be able to do their jobs quickly and safely.

Fire Safety

In schools, firefighters tell students to plan and practice **evacuation routes** at home with their families. They say, "Get low to the ground if there is smoke. Get out as quickly as you can. Meet your family members in a safe place outside."

1676	1725	1818
The first fire engine is used in the United States.	The ten-person water pump is invented for putting out fires.	Molly Williams, an African American slave, is the first female fire fighter.

Firefighters check fire safety at local businesses, too. They check their fire exits, fire **extinguishers**, and sprinklers. Firefighters need to be sure that businesses are safe for both the workers and the customers.

Firefighters help ➤ businesses keep their fire-safety equipment in good working order.

1872	1878	1890	1910
Automatic sprinklers are invented to put out fires inside large buildings.	The fire ladder is invented to reach tall buildings.	The fire escape ladder is invented.	The first gasoline powered fire engine with a power pump is invented.

Putting Out Fire

A fire needs three elements to burn: fuel, heat, and oxygen. To put out a fire, firefighters remove at least one of these elements. For example, they can smother a fire with a special foam so oxygen can't reach it. Or, firefighters can prevent these three elements from joining by clearing away dry brush so it won't become fuel for the fire.

1940s	1945	1950s	1974
Foam is used for the first time to put out fires.	Smokey the Bear is introduced as the symbol of forest fire prevention.	The air horn is introduced to sound alarms.	The first paid female firefighter, Judith Livers, is hired in Virginia.

When they go back to the station, firefighters take turns making their meals and doing the household chores.

Sometimes, firefighters give tours of the fire station. People learn about firefighting. They see where firefighters eat and sleep. The firefighters show people the equipment in the station and on the trucks. They might even show how the sirens work!

These firefighters show a school group how the fire equipment is used. ▼

Shopping for the Firehouse

Have you ever seen a fire truck parked at a supermarket? The firefighters are there shopping for groceries for their firehouse. They take the fire truck in case they have an emergency call. Every second counts in an emergency!

Fighting Fires

When an emergency call comes in, firefighters must be dressed and in the fire truck quickly. They stop whatever they're doing. They put their **bunker gear**, or protective gear, on over their clothes.

First they step into their boots and pull up their pants. Their boots are made of rubber and have steel toes. This protects them from nails, glass, and anything else that may fall on their feet.

Firefighters keep their protective pants rolled over their boots to save time in an emergency. ▼

▲ All firefighting gear is kept near the fire engine.

helmet

bunker gear
(coat)

gloves

bunker gear
(pants)

steel-toed
boots

17

Next they put on their jackets. Their clothes are **flame-retardant**. This reduces the heat in a fire and protects them from burns. Finally they put on their hats. They are made of hard plastic. This protects their heads if things fall during a fire.

The firefighters hop on the fire truck and rush to the fire. They turn on the siren and the red lights. The **air horn** warns cars to get out of the way. The **engineer** drives, and the captain rides up front. The firefighters ride in the back in the **jumpseat**.

Heavy!

When they are fighting fires, firefighters wear almost 100 pounds of protective gear.

▲ the engineer

911

In most areas of the United States, you can call 911 on a telephone when there is an emergency. The operator will contact the fire department for you.

Firefighters ▲ ride in the jumpseat.

When they get to the fire, firefighters put on special air tanks and breathing masks. This helps them breathe when the air is filled with smoke and fire.

Then, they hook big hoses from their fire truck to a **fire hydrant**. Two firefighters hold each hose. Sometimes, they need tall ladders to get to the fire. The truck carries ladders of all sizes.

Powerful!

Water comes out of the fire hose so fast and hard that it can knock down a grown man. That's why it takes two people to hold a hose steady.

When they go inside a burning building, firefighters work in a buddy system. Two firefighters stay together at all times. Their protective clothing may make them feel safer than they are. They can't feel the heat through their gear. They can't keep their eyes on everything all by themselves. So, they protect each other. They also have radios in their helmets so they can talk to the chief. The chief works to keep everyone safe.

Some firefighters search the building to make sure there are no people or animals inside. Their number-one job is rescue. Others put the fire out and try to save as much property as they can. Sometimes, they need to use tools like axes and electric saws.

The Wet Stuff

Before going into a fire, firefighters sometimes say, "Let's put the wet stuff on the red stuff!"

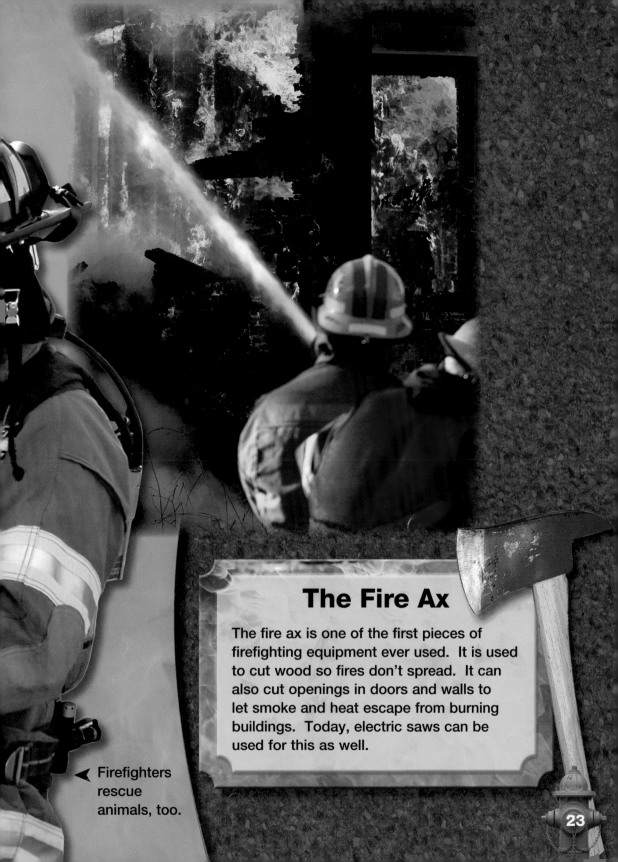

The Fire Ax

The fire ax is one of the first pieces of firefighting equipment ever used. It is used to cut wood so fires don't spread. It can also cut openings in doors and walls to let smoke and heat escape from burning buildings. Today, electric saws can be used for this as well.

◄ Firefighters rescue animals, too.

When the fire is out and the building is safe, firefighters let people know if and when they can reenter. The fire fighters pick up their things and head back to the station.

Home at Last

Back at the station, it's time to clean. The firefighters clean and check the equipment and trucks once again. They even clean the hoses. They need to clean themselves, too. They must be ready in case there is another emergency.

Finally they eat and relax if there is time before bed. If the alarm sounds, they'll have to rush out again. A firefighter's day is never really done.

Glossary

air horn—a loud horn or siren

bucket brigade—a firefighting method in which buckets of water are passed along a line

bunker gear—clothing that keeps the wearer safe from injuries such as burns

danger—something that is risky and may cause harm or loss

emergency—a strong need for assistance or help right away

engineer—the person who drives the fire engine

equipment—the supplies used to assist someone in doing a job

evacuation routes—plans for leaving a building in case of emergencies such as fires

extinguishers—equipment used to put out, or extinguish, fires by spraying them with a type of special foam

firefighters—people who fight fires as a job or as volunteers

fire hydrant—a pipe coming up from the ground where a hose can be attached and water can be drawn

flame-retardant—a type of material that keeps away, or resists, heat and burning

gauges—instruments that display levels

jumpseat—the seat that faces the rear of the fire truck

nozzles—ends of hoses from which the water is released

rescue—to free from danger

shift—a period of time during which a person is scheduled to work

Index